Sonja Carter

Simple Elegance Publishing
Wilmington, Delaware

Freedom In My Soul

Contact Sonja Carter at: capricemqg@yahoo.com

All Scripture quotations are from the King James Version of the Bible. (Public Domain).

Book Design and Layout by Ti Kendrick Randall
dotkconsulting@gmail.com
Photographs used with permission from
jupiterimages.com and inmagine.com

Poetry Is...

thoughts from the heart
birthed out of
a true spirit of worship
with a whisper

Table of Contents

Foreword

I have known Sonja since we were little girls. We have gone through many experiences together and through every season of our life we still remained friends.

I am truly excited that Sonja has finally taken her passion and talent to another level. The words on these pages will inspire, encourage, and empower you. This is her original work – authentic, unique, and birthed from within.

Sonja is a woman of integrity. Her sense of humor and passion has allowed her to persevere against all odds. She has come forth as pure gold. From playing in the projects to writing poems, Sonja's love for people has never changed. You won't understand the glory until you know her story.

Auanita Corley

Introduction

Years ago, God spoke to my spirit and said, "Your poetry is your way out of poverty." Full of unbelief at the time, I laughed and said, "Yeah, right." Years went on, as they do, whether you go forth in what God told you to do or not. In those years, my writing became important to me as I began to journal the affairs of my life.

I found writing to be an effective tool towards inner healing. These poems were written for healing and enjoyment – a little something to make you go "hmm..." As you read, reflect and allow God to minister to you. My prayer is that you will experience freedom in your soul.

John 8:36

"If the son therefore shall make you free, ye shall be free indeed."

For I reckon that the sufferings of this present time are not worthy to be compared with the glory which shall be revealed in us.

For the earnest expectation of the creature waiteth for the manifestation of the sons of God.

For the creature was made subject to vanity, not willingly, but by reason of him who hath subjected the same in hope,

Because the creature itself also shall be delivered from the

bondage

of corruption into the glorious liberty of the children of God.

Romans 8:18-21

Date Rape

"You better not tell a soul", he said
as he forced himself on top of me on the bed
I repeatedly told him "No!"
but instead of taking heed
he ripped off my clothes as if it were a sideshow,
indeed.

The rage in his eyes and the roughness in his voice,
in that moment I knew there was no choice.
Laying there stiff, staring at the ceiling –
it was like an out of body experience.

I was dead to my feelings

Violated and so exposed.
No way could I tell anyone,
so for years I kept it enclosed.
He was not a stranger.
Going out with him that night,
I didn't think my life was in danger.
How could I go on living, feeling so much shame?
All I wanted was to forget his name;
maybe it was just a game.

Could I possibly report this as being a rape?
After all, he was my charming date.
My view of sex was so perverted;
in order to enjoy it, thought a man had to hurt it.

After the ordeal was over, he walked me home;
up to my front door like nothing was wrong –
popping his fingers and singing a song.

I wrestled in my mind many years about that night.
The different events gave me stage fright.
How could a person be so cruel;
taking a girl's innocence like a foolish fool?

Battered

Sorry I hit you, babe. It won't happen again,
        he said.
However this came after he threw me across the bed.

"You made me upset, I thought you cared.
Just promise not to leave me, but always be there.

Let me see your face to kiss away your tears.
I am your man, no reason to fear.

You don't deserve to be slapped or pushed around.
You know I was going through something;
        my smile was upside down.

I love you so much, you are my best girl.
I just can't imagine living without you in this cold
        world.

Don't make me angry or pick a fight.
Things will work out if everyone is out of sight.

Really, I don't hit you that hard.
It's not like I threw you a mile or a yard.

I won't hit you again,
        he promised.
Please believe me, I am being honest.

We've been together so long where else can you go?
We have children – having someone else raise them
is definitely a "No-No."

Sorry, I hit you babe. It won't happen again.
Is it possible for us to be friends?

Better

When we first met, everything was fine;
had not a clue you would blow my mind.
We used to hold hands and walk through the park.
It was exciting; we were off to a peachy start.
My thoughts were with you daily,
never anticipating that you would fail me.

Then one day you hit me upside my head
and threw me violently across the bed.
My heart was pounding – felt only fear.
Couldn't scream, thought no one would hear.
I didn't perceive you were a violent, angry man;
my head was stuck deep in the sand.

That so-called love, I knew nothing about.
All I wanted was a way out.
It's over now, there is no looking back.
I must get healed and get my life on track.
We can't be friends or start over again.
The first time you hit me,
        our relationship should have ended.

You can no longer hurt me or make me cry.
The snare of the enemy has been broken;
        it's not my time to die.

The Secret

A *secret* cradled, couldn't open and share;
you wouldn't understand unless you'd been there.

I felt awful after the *abortion*;
felt like a part of me was missing a great fortune.
At times I would sit and think about
what it would have been...
A boy or a girl, fat – maybe thin.
Whose features would he or she have had?
– Mom's or maybe even Dad's.

counting the birthdays
was the hardest part.
The years were embedded, etched in my heart.
Haunted by a baby's cry every night;
battling in my soul until daylight.

forgiving myself
was a major task.
I wanted to crawl under a rock
and put the abortion in the past.
Now the secret is out, no longer do I hide.

No, *never haunted again*
by my baby's cry.

The Divorce

My heart was broken after the divorce.
My "Knight In Shining Armor" galloped away
  on his horse.
Feelings of failure eroded my mind;
the love of my life had seemed so kind.

Staring out the window,
wondering what he did with all
  the personal information I shared;
felt like he played me and didn't really care.
He'd seen me without a façade
and
awakened parts of my soul I didn't realize was inside.
When we were together, sparkles were in my eyes –
but now feeling jilted, like it was all lies.

Thought he was the answer to my prayers –
someone to stick with me through life's basic cares.
He was a hand to hold on a cold winter night
and a shoulder to cry on when I felt uptight.
My mate was gone and I didn't want to live;
felt like I had nothing left to give.
I cried so much, my emotions were shattered;
  for days, weeks, and months
I was depressed and nothing mattered.

A Mother's Cry

Rising up early before the crack of dawn
to spend time in prayer before the sound of the alarm.

Rushing to work to make ends meet,
barely having time to rest my feet.

Waiting for payday to handle my bills.
I'm hoping enough oil is in the tank to
    prevent us from chills.

Kids acting up in school
    – don't want to obey the rules.
I'm feeling perplexed because they were not raised
    to be fools.

Teacher, mentor, and nurse – just to name a few.
A mother's job is more than sitting in a pew.

I thought about going home to take a nap,
    a twenty-minute one, as a matter of fact.
But there was dinner to be made by no later than six.
If we were going to eat, I had to get in the mix.

I know you've heard of meals on wheels;
but mothers have ways of creating miracle meals
    by using no frills.

Managing a household with my bare hands;

sometimes collecting empty soda cans.

It's not always easy to stop and sigh…
this may not be your story,
but it's a mother's cry.

The Streets

the streets seems to have a voice of their own
drawing our sons
luring them away from home
drugs and violence negative tools
a trap to put them in solitary confinement

boys hanging on the corners
getting high
moving in slow motion like professional mourners
gun-shots fired
innocent victims in pain
perpetrators acting like life is a game

police brutality
the system is a maze
as anger hovers over the city like a haze
politicians all baffled
no answers in sight
trying to understand
what makes the youth continue to fight

the streets seem to have a voice of its own
trying to lure our sons away from home

Wounded

A wounded spirit, a broken heart
thirsting trying to find a new start

Love comes in different sizes and shades
life at times is such a maze

Men and women tossed and torn
some wishing they were never born

Hoping and seeking to find help

not knowing that the answer is right up above
a gift from God, His eternal love.

If Only

if only I was given a chance
not rejection
of human affection
leading only to mental depression
a product of my environment
a cursed reflection
left fending for myself
          without protection
drinking and drugs were all a part of my life's game
that's how my family coped in order to maintain
education was barely talked about
but I know inwardly it was a positive way out
if only I was given a chance for my hopes and dreams
to come alive
to escape the haunting feelings of wanting to die
if only...

Bored

Have you ever been so bored you could cry?
talking to yourself, of course, there was no reply.
So bored with doing the same job
singing the same song
dull as an old bell ringing – ding dong.
Tired of the same old scene,
wishing you could go and watch a movie screen.

Bored with the comforts and familiar places in life
Bored out of your mind, you just want to fight
Bored beyond what you can really explain
feeling like you're going insane

Have you ever been so bored you could…?

Inside Me

for

so long

I danced to everyone else's beat
while inwardly dying,
battling with defeat

afraid

to stand up for what I believed feeling tossed aside,
like an unwanted seed
My real beauty I could barely see
because I always pondered
what others thought about me
I never thought anything I did was good enough
my life felt so

empty

how could I reach for the stars
when my mind was confused and

trapped

by bars?
nowhere to run
nowhere to hide
echoes of a

little girl

screaming inside

For I reckon that the sufferings of this present time are not worthy to be compared with the glory which shall be revealed in us.

For the earnest expectation of the creature waiteth for the manifestation of the sons of God.

For the creature was made subject to vanity, not willingly, but by reason of him who hath subjected the same in hope,

Because the creature itself also shall be delivered from the bondage of corruption into the glorious

liberty

of the children of God.

Romans 8:18-21

Men...

Don't walk around in despair
not knowing who you are;
in Jesus' eyes you are a star.
He created you to **be strong**
in the power of His might
realizing that life is a spiritual fight.
He has given you dominion over the land
to fulfill His purpose
and **carry out His plan**.
Drugs and violence is not the key.
Come to Jesus
and He will set you free.
God's love for you is unconditional.
He doesn't see you as you are,
but as you can be.
We need you all across the nation
to be leaders and positive role models
for the future generations.

Men...

In Him
you will find all you need
to live and succeed.

A Father's Touch

As a young girl, I longed for my father to say
"Baby girl, I am proud of you."
I longed for him to hold me in his loving arms
and wipe away my many tears.
My soul needed that special touch that
only a father could give.
I always knew that if Dad was around,
he would make me feel
like a queen with a crown.
I just wanted him to love me just as I was
didn't matter to me the cost.
I would imagine in my mind
the walks and talks we would share;
my hopes and dreams I would bare.
He is the vine, I am the branch.
Daddy was my hero
any other man beside him was a zero.
Oh yes, my Daddy is one of a kind;
when he is with me, he is all mine.

Dear Jesus

Dear Jesus,
Hear me as I pray.
Help me as I walk this Christian way.
Lead and guide me so that I may see those things
        You have ordained for me.
Help me to keep my mind on You
        because that's the only way to make it through.

Dear Jesus,
Once again, I pray,
help me walk this Christian way.

A Prayer For You

I said a prayer for you today
that God would bless you in every way.
May you be guided by His loving hand.
Let His Word be the light of your path
leading and directing in those time of distress.
Yes, I said a prayer for you today
that God would bless you in every way.

A Place Of My Own

Solitude and refuge from the pressures of life,
a moment of silence aboard a new flight.

Somewhere I can let myself go
and hear the sound of the rivers flow.

Leaving behind the world and its cares
to enjoy a peaceful atmosphere.

A time of relaxation
to escape every day frustrations.

To put my mind at ease
and focus on my hopes and dreams.

Getting away for some time alone,
just to have a place of my own.

In Time

In time
things will come to pass
just pray, wait and be steadfast.

In time
you will see God knows what is best
just stand on His Word and endure your test.

In time
my child, you will see
just how special you are to Me.

Just As I Am

to You, I run with every secret
at Your feet is where I get naked
and bare all
the way You hold me in Your bosom
and wipe away my tears
You comfort me
in You I find security
You lift me up when I am down
through You, strength I have found
to You I run; hasten to Your throne

Lover of my soul…

Redeemer of my life…

Healer of all my hurts…

A Rainbow

The many phases
of love
and the different paths
of life
that lead to a brighter future
with endless
possibilities

Snowflakes

Snowflakes falling
so pure and white
visions of diamonds
a dazzling sight
they fall from the sky
not making a sound
yet evidence of them are all on the ground
Snowflakes falling
hitting my face
reminds me of winter
and times of embrace
They are big and some are small
it's a miracle if you can count them all

Winter

Winter is here
you can tell by the bare trees
and the air from the cold breeze

People are dressed warm from head to toe
hearts singing
"Let it snow. Let it snow."

Winter is here
the air is crisp
everything around
so still and stiff

Alone But Not Lonely

Singleness brings about isolation
and battles of loneliness
Singleness is a seasonal process
Winter is the season of intimacy that brings one
into a level of self-awareness
Spring is the season of learning to love yourself
and going through the growing pains of maturity
        the embracing of new life
Summer is planning time alone
celebrating yourself
enduring the journey of being single
Fall is like the transformation of a lump of clay
marred in the potter's hand
being made over again
with a new outlook on life
It's a stage where all things fall off that are not
necessary
        for the next level in life.
So whatever season you find yourself in,
remember that being single is having a
whole-hearted
love affair with yourself
being alone, but not lonely
knowing
that you are not qualified to be with anyone else
until you are qualified to be with yourself.

A Love Letter

You were in my thoughts so hard today;
thought about how special you are in every way.
I remember the day you were born,
even before the earth was formed.
The times you were hurt and pushed aside
I felt your pain
I knew you couldn't see me with your physical eyes.
Yet, I was constantly praying that your love for me
would never die.
You have been through some trying times
when most people would have given up
at the drop of a dime.
You are my love;
keep believing your deliverance is nigh.

In Love

I was afraid to love again
until I met you.
Building a friendship was all so new.
Let's try not to take this relationship so fast
because this is a love that I want to last.
Love is something special
not just a fling
it's emotions going deep down inside
that makes your soul sing

You think of ways to express how you feel
something unique
for a love that's so real.
We will have ups and downs
because no relationship is perfect.
But as long as there's love between us
it will all be worth it.

Our love will stand the test of time
it's like a ruby, rare to find.
The fear that was once there is now gone
and replaced by hopes that our love will carry on.

Shame

I had no knowledge
shame was such a dirty game
inwardly draining,
    trying to make me insane.

Sometimes I would beat up on myself so bad
thinking I was a victim, left lonely and sad.

Shame was so much a part of my world
always reminding me I was a bad girl.

No longer bound by shame

Hip no more to the game
free indeed…
devil you are under my feet
    – in *Jesus'* Name.

Affirmation

Affirmation was something I sought after from others
Shame, intimidation, and unforgiveness
    these were my peers.
Keeping me captive, living in fear.
It was a struggle growing up.
I always felt less than, dwelling on my faults.
My growth was stunted, not knowing who I was.
    – a woman walking around with no clue.

Positive things I had to speak into my life
A task so hard, an uncomfortable flight.
Then one day, I was introduced to a man.
One that held answers in His hand.
He began to teach me about myself,
    treasures that were hidden inside on a shelf.
Piece by piece they were brought to light
this was my battle I had to fight
I kept on searching for those treasures inside;
I just couldn't give up
    because at the end was the victor's cup.
It took a lot of soul searching for me to see
that what was missing lay dormant inside me.

Rise

Lord, here I am again
no longer can I hide myself behind fear
For my ears hear, my blessing is so near…
so near…

Come, My daughter,
break out of fear.
your destiny awaits…
rise to the occasion
embrace your place of wealth
enter your land of promise
fear no longer has dominion over you

Be Strong

strength is not measured
by one's ability to move
swiftly
but to endure the race
to conquer every obstacle
to face every fear
with confidence in the things not seen

standing against all odds
waiting patiently
for the manifestation of the promise

strength is not something you were born with
but an inheritance from God, Himself
after all, He commands us
to be Strong
and of good courage
not to be afraid
nor be dismayed
for the Lord, your God, is with you
wherever you go.

End of Life

The end of this life is not the end of the road;
but an open door to the streets of gold.
Where there will be no more
crying
or dying
or sickness…

Angels encamped all around the throne saying,
"Holy, Holy, Holy, is the Lord God Almighty."
Eternal life
everlasting joy
a free spirit
            that has no limit or chains of bondage.
Life anew
never perishing;
engulfed in the presence of our God,
hands continuously lifted up in praise.

Where mortal has put on immortality
and has ceased from all trouble.
Living with the Lover of Your Soul
always fruitful and never growing old.
Knowing that your life has just begun
in another dimension
and a far greater existence
Living
to live again.

Direction

Order my steps in Your Word.
I need direction
my life is in your hands
show me the pathway of life
you hold my future – everything is alright.
Keep my head lifted up
my shield
my strength
as the struggle continues deep within.
I'm standing on Your Word, a strong foundation,
Your spoken Word brought about creation
my faith in You
is all I have sometimes
fragile
like a piece of glass.
You are the potter; I'm the clay
        mold me in every way.
Order my steps for the rest of my life.
My Creator
My Friend
I trust you with all my might.

Angels

Angels, ascending and descending,
sent to watch over me
I feel the brush of their wings
the Glory is all over
Angels, ascending and descending,
sent to watch over me
protecting me from harm
keeping me safe from all alarm

Preach

The preached word is like a
counseling session
sitting at the foot of Jesus
getting your spirit edified
and your mind
renewed.

Destiny

destiny is a chosen,
pre-determined,
ordained place
for something
already formed before the foundation
of the world
an expected end
orchestrated by God
one appointment that you will arrive to
in your time of completion
destiny is being brought to perfection,
fulfillment,
and contentment
looking unto Jesus
who is the Author and Finisher of your faith
Reaching your full potential
standing strong
knowing
that you are a seed
predestined
for greatness

Just A Glimpse

God showed me a glimpse today
just a peek of the future
things came together, the crooked path was straight

In the glimpse, was such an awesome light
there was a sense of peace
a place of fulfillment
that went beyond what I could see

A glimpse of the future
that came with such speed
letting me know not to fret, but to take heed
things seemed so close and tangible
just one touch away
something so awesome
couldn't let this slip away

God was showing me things that are to come in time
just a glimpse of treasures
He has in mind
He showed me just a glimpse today
that allowed me to see life in a unique way

My Scented Candle

The fire that burns within
vapors of love with an eternal end

A light that shines through the windows of my soul
the sunshine it brings to a spirit that is cold
A flame of peace that flickers
in the midst of a storm
one of serenity with a wholesome warmth

The aroma it sends out so sweet and so pure
scents of glory so full and so free
filled with essence of love
churning on the inside of me

A light that shines standing on its own
a witness to others that you are not alone

Women Walking Together In Unity

Women coming together
from all walks of life
striving to be one
in the Body of Christ.
Going through things that are similar
but not exactly alike,
yet having compassion for one another –
enduring the fight.
Tearing down the walls of jealously
that have kept us apart
building bridges of love
coming from the heart.
Being transformed,
what a challenging task,
overcoming the wounds and hurts of the past.
Women walking together in unity
standing strong
reaching our full potential
pressing to battle on
we are more than conquerors
destined to succeed
because of the liberty we have in Christ
we are destined to be set free.

Only The Strong Survive

Trials and tribulations are vital to our growth
they are vehicles used to aid us in being
more than conquerors.
It's through our life experiences that we obtain
perception;
sometimes, the way we see our problems
is the problem –
we need a change of lens.
To accomplish true victory
requires wisdom in choosing
          which battles to fight.
Not every question will be answered in this lifetime.
Some things are just out of our control,
mishaps often happen,
it can be mind-boggling trying to understand
things in the natural world.
You become bewildered
living in the "what if's" depletes your soul
from having joy and peace.
Evil forces war against God's plan of making us
strong and prosperous.

...Just hold on...

Strength is not measured by your ability
to move swiftly
but to endure the race
facing every fear with confidence

in the things not seen
stand
against all odds
wait for the manifestation of your promise.
A process that will develop a fervent spirit
that will sustain you.
You can make it because
only the strong survive.

Restoration

rising up and out of the grave
possessing wealth
taking dominion over your territory
thoughts altered into another realm
a spiritual height
discernment made keen
seeing far beyond the natural
strength renewed as an eagle
a place of contentment with such tranquility
a newness
a fresh start
definitely a new dawn
a season of reimbursement
resting in the blessing of the Lord
your latter end more fruitful than your beginning
restoration is rediscovering and redefining yourself
as a whole person:
body
soul
and spirit

A Mother's Love

No one can take the place of a mother.
She is someone special
and can't be compared to another.
She is one who is always there
to help you through life's despair
There were times she had to make decisions
that seemed mean and unfair.
But deep in her heart, she really cared.

And as you take a moment's rest,
you will understand that she did what was best.
Think of the things she has endured,
the pain of birth,
to bring you forth on God's green earth.
The sacrifices that she makes,
aiding her family, doing what it takes.

When you were sick in the middle of the night,
she sat up nursing you until daylight.
Putting her hopes and dreams on hold
to raise her children, giving them a loving home.
Making sure you were properly clothed and fed.
Sometimes reading a story before tucking you in bed.

Nothing can take the place of a mother's love,
it's something unconditional that comes from above.

Just Your Face

When I wake in the morning at sunrise

I just want to see your face.

No conversation
(nor hesitation)

I just want to see your face

Before I go to sleep at night
after battling the hustle and bustle
of another day's fight

I just want to see your face

No masquerades or charades

just...
your face...

MeMe's Baby

The inducing of your birth
caused labor to be so long
you were born premature
yet very strong
all ten toes and fingers were in place
it brought joy to my heart looking at
your beautiful face
Your heart was beating at its normal rate
the presence that filled the room was free from hate
Everything was ready for your arrival
a baby shower was thrown
to celebrate your survival
Your cry was a sign of life
a signal to all, "I'm ready to take flight."
Family and friends were waiting
for the announcement of your birth
a call to know that you were on this earth
As your mother held you tightly in her arms
I gave thanks to God for keeping you from harm
Your life, I'Niyah, is so blessed
because you are one of God's best.
MeMe will always have a special place in her heart
  for you
and a prayer that God will bless you
  your whole life through

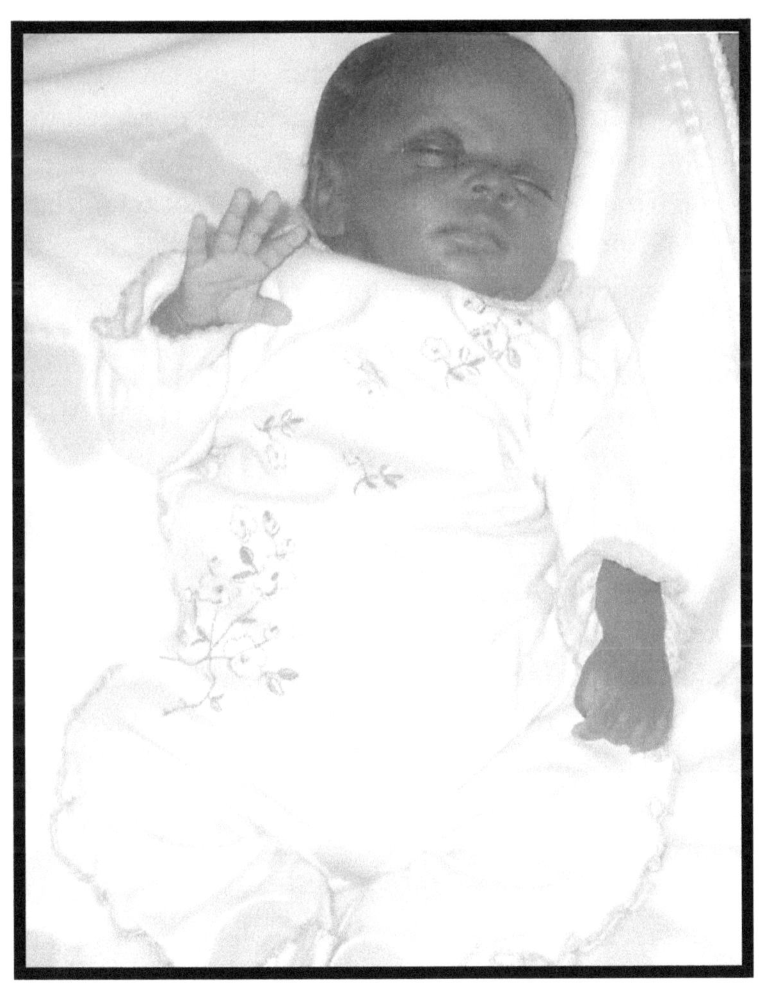

Acknowledgements

My deepest gratitude goes first to Jesus Christ, the Lover and Healer I've longed for all my life. Thank You, Jesus – for believing in me even when I didn't believe in myself.

Thanks to my children Iyeshia, Marketa, Mark and Marvin for encouraging me. Remember, after all is said and done, I just want to see your faces.

To my granddaughter, I'Niyah – you will always be MeMe's baby. I also say "Thank you" to my siblings, nieces and nephews for all of your support.

I thank my parents Carroll Lee and Nettie Carter for raising me in the way I should go.

"Thank you" to the world's greatest friends a woman could have: Dee, Auanita, Carol, Stella and Deshawn – you are all the best. Love Ya!

I thank my spiritual mothers: Pastor Mercedes Anthony, Pastor Phyllis Rose, Pastor Sharon Ryan and Ms. Marlene Aiken. Thanks for giving me godly wisdom.

Last, but not least, I thank my Pastors: Shannon and First Lady Nikki McNeil, of Grace Camp Fellowship Ministries (Kingdom Harvest Ministries). This poetry book was in me for years; however, I needed a midwife to bring it forth. Thank you for being true vessels of God. He will not forget your labor of love.

Sonja Carter grew up in the projects of Riverside and graduated from Glasgow High School in 1984 with training in Child Care.

Freedom In My Soul is her first published body of work. Sonja is concerned about the well-being of others – in body, mind, soul, and spirit. She has had the honor of performing her poetry at several churches and women's conferences.

Ms. Carter is also a licensed Evangelist at Grace Camp Fellowship Ministries, under the leadership of Pastor Shannon McNeil.

Sonja has an extensive employment history with children and teens. She currently works for Positive Directions as a "Time Out" Interventionist.

She is a single mother of four – two girls, and two boys – and a MeMe of one granddaughter. She resides in Wilmington, Delaware.

www.ingramcontent.com/pod-product-compliance
Ingram Content Group UK Ltd.
Pitfield, Milton Keynes, MK11 3LW, UK
UKHW041839200726
13854UKWH00003BA/1228